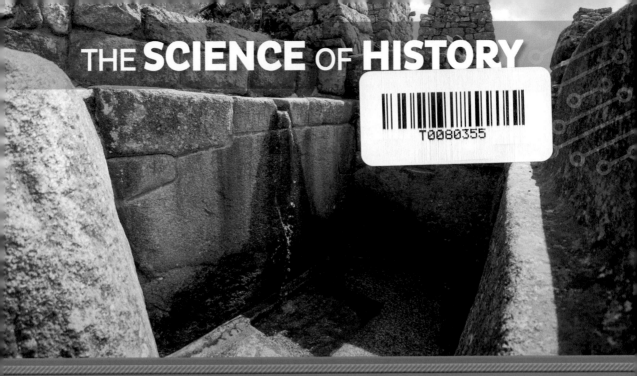

THE SCIENCE OF HISTORY

SCIENCE OF MACHU PICCHU

by Golriz Golkar

CAPSTONE PRESS
a capstone imprint

Capstone Captivate is published by Capstone Press, an imprint of Capstone.
1710 Roe Crest Drive
North Mankato, Minnesota 56003
capstonepub.com

Library of Congress Cataloging-in-Publication Data
Names: Golkar, Golriz, author.
Title: Science of Machu Picchu / Golriz Golkar.
Description: North Mankato, Minnesota : Capstone Press, [2023] | Series: The science of history | Includes bibliographical references and index. | Audience: Ages 8–11 | Audience: Grades 4–6 | Summary: "Have you ever heard of Machu Picchu? It's an ancient citadel high in the mountains of Peru. Science played a big role in the building of Machu Picchu and the daily life of the Inca people who lived there. Find out the science behind Machu Picchu. Discover how modern technology is being used to uncover more mysteries of this ancient place"—Provided by publisher.
Identifiers: LCCN 2021056943 (print) | LCCN 2021056944 (ebook) | ISBN 9781666334906 (hardcover) | ISBN 9781666334913 (paperback) | ISBN 9781666334920 (pdf) | ISBN 9781666334944 (kindle edition)
Subjects: LCSH: Machu Picchu Site (Peru)—Juvenile literature. | Science, Ancient—Peru—Machu Picchu Site—Juvenile literature. | Incas—History—Juvenile literature.
Classification: LCC F3429.1.M3 G65 2023 (print) | LCC F3429.1.M3 (ebook) | DDC 985/.37—dc23/eng/20220126
LC record available at https://lccn.loc.gov/2021056943
LC ebook record available at https://lccn.loc.gov/2021056944

Editorial Credits

Editor: Erika L. Shores; Designer: Heidi Thompson; Media Researcher: Jo Miller; Production Specialist: Tori Abraham

Image Credits

Alamy: Lordprice Collection, 7, (Top), mauritius images GmbH, 20, North Wind Picture Archives, 37, Photo 12, 35; Getty Images: AFP, 30, Dorling Kindersley, 32, duncan1890, 27, Markus Daniel, 18, 43, Nivek Neslo, 44, PytyCzech, 17 (globe, insets); Science Source: GeoEye, 12; Shutterstock: Andrei Metelev, 29, astudio, 38, Avim Wu, 7, (Bottom), BlueRingMedia, 26, cge2010, 5, ChrisW, 33, Craig Hastings, Cover, (Bottom), Desiree Sessegolo, 25, Fabio Lamanna, 42, KamimiArt (design element), Kavic.C, 13, legacy1995, 14, Maksimushkina Olga, 15, Matyas Rehak, 41, Nasky, 31, notsuperstar, 19, olenadesign, 6, Rainer Lesniewski, 21, Sandro Sandoval, Cover (Top), 1, SL-Photography, 22, Soleil Nordic, 17 (chart), steve estvanik, 8, vitmark, 11, WH_Pics, 28, Yasemin Olgunoz Berber, 24, Zenobillis, 45

All internet sites appearing in back matter were available and accurate when this book was sent to print.

TABLE OF CONTENTS

Words in **bold** text are included in the glossary.

CHAPTER 1

A HIDDEN CITADEL

Imagine waking up early one morning in Cuzco, Peru. You take your backpack and begin a journey. You follow a winding trail in the Andes Mountains. You pass through green forests and climb grassy mountaintops. You follow stone steps and tunnels carved in rock hundreds of years ago.

After four days of hiking, you arrive at an ancient stone gate. As you pass through it, the morning fog slowly disappears. The ruins of a walled **citadel** appear. They sit high on a mountain ridge. The crumbling walls and steps blend in with the landscape. So many questions fill your mind. This was a place where people had once lived. But who were they? When did they live there? Where did they go? Science helped build this place and it can help answer your questions.

Clouds often cover the ancient citadel because of its location high in the Andes Mountains.

AN ANCIENT INCA SETTLEMENT

Through careful digging called **excavation**, scientists know that this is Machu Picchu. It is located about 50 miles (80 kilometers) northwest of Cuzco. Using scientific methods, the Inca people built this settlement during the mid-1400s. They also paved the Inca Trail that leads from Cuzco to the site.

The Inca empire was the largest and most powerful of its time. It was based in Cuzco and stretched from modern-day Argentina to southern Colombia. However, the empire only lasted just over 100 years. Spanish conquerors and disease wiped out the Incas by the 1570s.

Plants grew over Machu Picchu. For hundreds of years, it was known mostly by the locals. In 1911, a professor named Hiram Bingham stumbled upon the site while looking for another city.

Hiram Bingham

The Inca Road

Many parts of the 24,000-mile (39,000-km) Inca Road still exist today. It links six countries in South America. The Inca Trail is the most well-known part of the road. It is about 25 miles (40 km) long.

Most Inca cities were destroyed by the Spanish. Machu Picchu was left in place. The citadel's remote location kept it hidden. To this day, no one knows for sure why it was built and abandoned. The Incas had no written language. They left no records of their history.

Scientists and historians have found some clues to these mysteries. The way the citadel was built shows the style and taste of the Inca **emperor** Pachacuti. He ruled from about 1438 to 1471. The emperor played a major role in expanding Inca lands.

Most experts believe Pachacuti likely built Machu Picchu as royal property. The emperor, his family, **nobility**, and servants lived there. Members of the nobility included priests and military and government leaders. They helped run the empire. They collected taxes and enforced laws. Through scientific discoveries, mysteries of this ancient site have slowly been unraveled.

Between Two Peaks

The settlement lies between the peaks of the Machu Picchu and Huayna Picchu Mountains and covers 80,000 acres (32,400 hectares) of land. It rests 7,970 feet (2,429 meters) above sea level on the eastern slope of the Andes Mountains. It overlooks the Urubamba River below. Machu Picchu means "Old Peak" and Huayna Picchu means "New Peak" in the Quechua language spoken by the Incas.

CHAPTER 2

BUILDING MACHU PICCHU

By studying Machu Picchu's remains, scientists learned the Incas were skilled builders. Science also helped the Incas expand their empire. They used their scientific knowledge to build roads and bridges.

To build sites such as Machu Picchu, the Incas were masters at stonemasonry. First, they collected granite rocks from the ground or the mountains. Chisels or wooden wedges were used to **quarry** rock from the mountains. The Incas built their structures without the help of wheels or animals. No iron or steel tools have ever been found. They moved stones and built everything by hand.

Fact

Many of the stones that were used to build the city weigh more than 50 pounds (23 kilograms).

Lighter stones were probably tumbled. Heavier stones were pushed or dragged. To shape rocks, the Incas used river cobblestones as hammerstones. The largest were used to cut and shape rocks for building. Medium-sized hammerstones smoothed stone faces. Small hammerstones smoothed stone corners. Lastly, the stones were carefully fit together without using mortar. Even a knife blade could not slide between them! Machu Picchu has remained mostly intact for more than 500 years. Even the area's many earthquakes have not brought it down!

A wall at Machu Picchu shows how well the stones were fit together by Inca stonemasons.

BUILDING IN EARTHQUAKE TERRITORY

Machu Picchu is built on two faults. These are cracks in the earth's surface where movement occurs. Sometimes, pressure builds up along a fault. When it is released suddenly, energy waves ripple underground. This movement is called an earthquake.

A satellite image of Machu Picchu (center) and its surrounding areas

Satellite images taken from space show underground cracks below Machu Picchu. Satellites take pictures of something from different angles. This creates an image with depth. Scientists saw that the citadel was built on the spot where the two faults meet. They wondered why the citadel was built in an earthquake zone. Recent research has shown the Incas likely did this on purpose. Earthquakes created many cracked rocks below the site. That meant these rocks were easy to cut for building.

The citadel walls point in the direction of the faults. The faults directed rainwater toward the city. The cracks below the surface allowed water to drain properly. The Incas' stonework also kept structures from toppling. During an earthquake, these stones bounce and fall back into place. Surprisingly, Machu Picchu's location in an earthquake zone is a main reason why it still stands today.

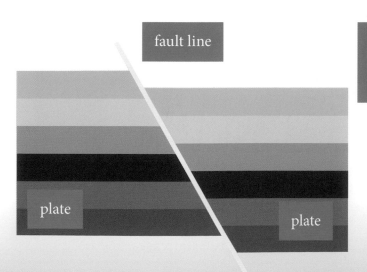

fault line

plate

plate

An earthquake occurs when two plates move at a fault line.

THE TEMPLE OF THE SUN

Scientists noticed Machu Picchu's largest buildings face mountains considered holy by the Incas. The Incas believed in many nature gods. They especially honored the sun god, Inti. They believed Inti sent his children to Earth to help humankind. The Inca emperor believed he was a direct **descendant** of Inti. He held ceremonies in temples to honor the movements of the sun and the moon.

Emperor Pachacuti

Fact
Machu Picchu has more than 200 buildings and 100 staircases.

One of the most important places at Machu Picchu is the Temple of the Sun. It was likely used to track seasons. This helped the Incas plan farming practices. Seasons change because Earth revolves around the sun on a tilted axis. Different parts of the planet receive more or less sunlight throughout the year.

During each season, light filters differently through the windows of the Temple of the Sun.

Twice a year, Earth's axis is tilted most closely to the sun. These two days are called a solstice. They happen on the first day of winter and summer. When it is winter on one side of the world, it is summer on the other side. The winter solstice is the day of the year with the least amount of sunlight. The summer solstice is the day with the most. On the first day of fall and spring, the sun shines directly above the equator. These two days are called an equinox. On an equinox, day and night are of equal length.

Machu Picchu's Temple of the Sun has a large stone inside. On the summer solstice, sunlight shines through a window and on to one side of this stone. The light lines up with the stone and the tip of a nearby mountain peak. On this day, the Incas knew it was the start of planting season.

On the fall equinox, sunlight shines through the twin peaks of the nearby mountain. This marked the start of the harvest. The Incas likely planned their farming schedule by following the temple's sunlight patterns.

Machu Picchu is located in the southern hemisphere. When it is fall there, it is spring in the northern hemisphere.

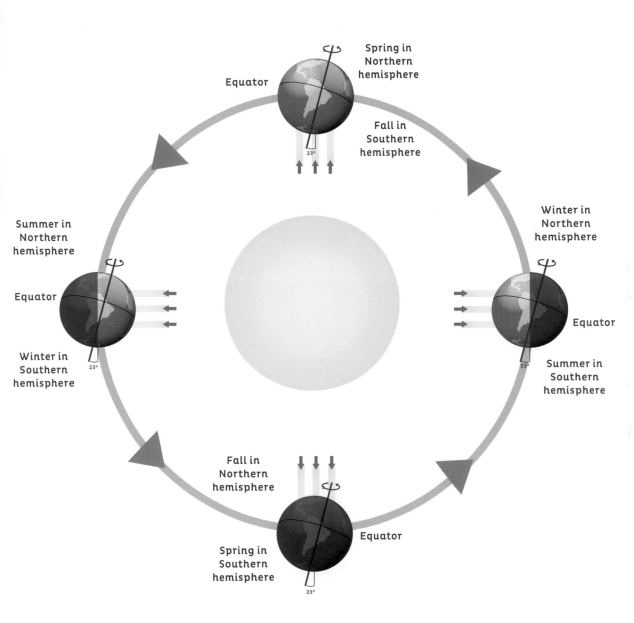

CHAPTER 3

LIFE AT THE CITADEL

In one area of Machu Picchu, rows of stone houses were surrounded by courtyards. Servants and nobility lived and worked here. Stone storehouses are found nearby. The Incas used them to store and protect food.

Large stone buildings such as this one were built by the Incas to store food and keep it from rotting.

Heat and moisture can cause **microorganisms** such as bacteria and fungi to break down nutrients in food. This process makes food rot. The Incas built storehouses in shady and breezy areas. This helped keep food cool and dry. They also cut holes into storehouse roofs and built drainage canals. These measures helped keep water from reaching food and improved airflow. The Incas could store foods such as corn, potatoes, and grains for many months.

To keep meat fresh, they used a freeze-drying process. They dried meat in hot daytime and cold nighttime temperatures. This removed its water and kept it safe to eat for months.

Fact

The word "jerky" comes from the Quechua word "chárki" for freeze-dried meat.

Mold is a fungus that grows when potatoes rot.

The emperor lived in another section of the citadel. His home included a garden, kitchen, and private bathroom. The citadel's **aqueduct** system gave the emperor easy water access.

Water runs through a stone aqueduct.

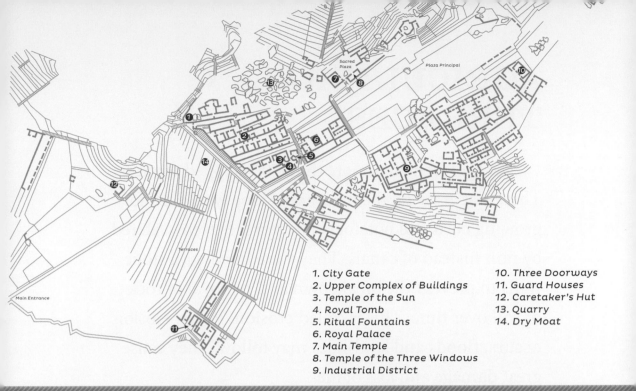

Sacred Plaza

Plaza Principal

Main Entrance

Terraces

1. City Gate
2. Upper Complex of Buildings
3. Temple of the Sun
4. Royal Tomb
5. Ritual Fountains
6. Royal Palace
7. Main Temple
8. Temple of the Three Windows
9. Industrial District
10. Three Doorways
11. Guard Houses
12. Caretaker's Hut
13. Quarry
14. Dry Moat

Before building the site, the Incas located a spring on the northern slope of Machu Picchu Mountain. From there, they built a stone aqueduct to carry water toward the citadel. Some of the water flowed to 16 stone fountains around the site. The first fountain was built next to the emperor's home. He was given first access to water.

Cloud Forests

Machu Picchu lies in a tropical cloud forest. Cloud forests are found high in the mountains. The cloud cover creates constant humidity and periods of heavy rainfall. This allows plants to grow and supplies local rivers with water.

AGRICULTURAL TERRACES

Machu Picchu has more than 700 stepped terraces. These flat areas on the mountain slope were used for growing corn and potatoes. The terraces were watered by rain instead of canals. They were lined with stone walls to prevent the breakdown and removal of rock or soil over time. This is called erosion. When erosion occurs, floods and landslides may follow. They cause great damage and loss of life.

Grass grows on the terraces of Machu Picchu today.

Scientists discovered the terrace soil was carefully layered to prevent erosion. The bottom layer had large stones and gravel. The middle layer was made up of sandy dirt. Rich topsoil made up the top layer. Topsoil contains weathered rocks and decomposed matter. Decomposition happens when bacteria and fungi break down dead plants or animals into simpler forms. Soil sucks up nutrients from this material that help plants grow. The stone walls and layered soil helped drain water properly. Without this clever terrace design, the citadel would have eroded long ago.

Fact

Modern research has found that the terraces could not have produced enough food for the whole population. Farming was likely also done in the nearby hills.

THE ARTIFACTS

Scientists have discovered many ceramic jars, plates, and pots at Machu Picchu. These daily items from long ago are called artifacts. Inca pottery was mostly made from clay. It was either shaped by hand or made with a mold. Then it was painted and decorated before being fired.

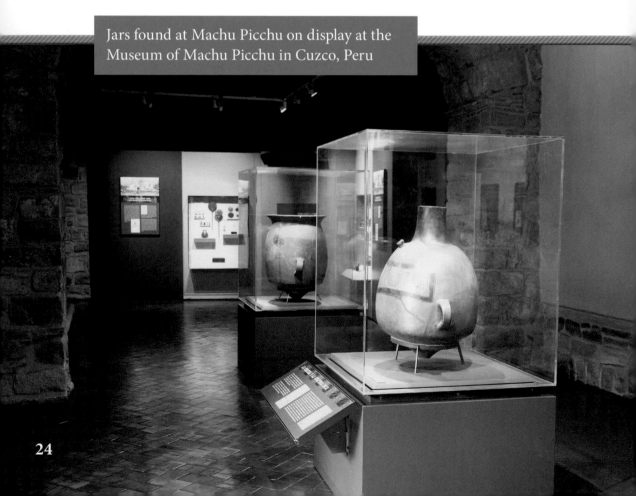

Jars found at Machu Picchu on display at the Museum of Machu Picchu in Cuzco, Peru

The Inca people knew the temperature of the fire played a part in the color of their ceramics.

The Incas understood the science behind making pottery that would last. The process they used also brought out bold, lasting colors in the painted decorations on the pottery. Ceramics are fired to dry and harden the clay. Fire needs oxygen to burn. As the fire heats up, compounds in the clay or the painted surface burn off. Oxygen rushes in. This creates brightly colored ceramics. If the oxygen supply is reduced instead, the fire doesn't burn completely. In this way, dark-colored ceramics are created.

Ceramic jars likely held chicha. This was a popular Incan drink. It was usually made from corn.

Science was involved in the process of making chicha as well. First, corn had to be chewed and spit out. After it dried, it was mixed with boiling water. Then it was pressed and strained to remove the liquid from the corn. Next, the liquid was poured into a closed jar. The liquid was left to ferment for several days. Fermentation is a chemical process. Molecules such as glucose are broken down by bacteria or a fungus called yeast. The warmth and moisture of a closed jar creates yeast growth. Chicha was made when the yeast broke down the corn sugars into alcohol.

The Fermentation Process

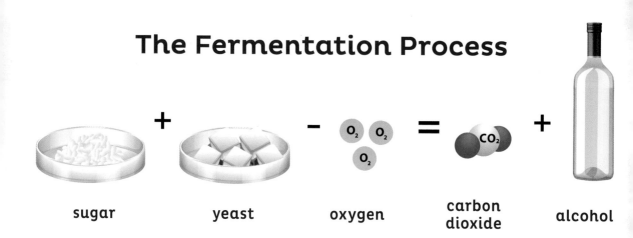

sugar + yeast − oxygen = carbon dioxide + alcohol

An illustration from the 1800s shows people in Peru drinking chicha.

The Incas were also skilled at metalwork. They used a process called metallurgy. It turned metal into useful objects. Tools used for making metal items such as hammers and molds have been found at the site.

Many bronze objects have also been discovered. Bronze is made of copper and tin. It is an alloy. An alloy is a type of metal made by combining two or more other types of metal elements. These elements make the object stronger. They also keep it from wearing down or rusting. This makes the objects last longer. Bronze tools, bowls, and jewelry are among the artifacts scientists have discovered.

A bronze knife made by the Inca people has the shape of a llama's head on the handle.

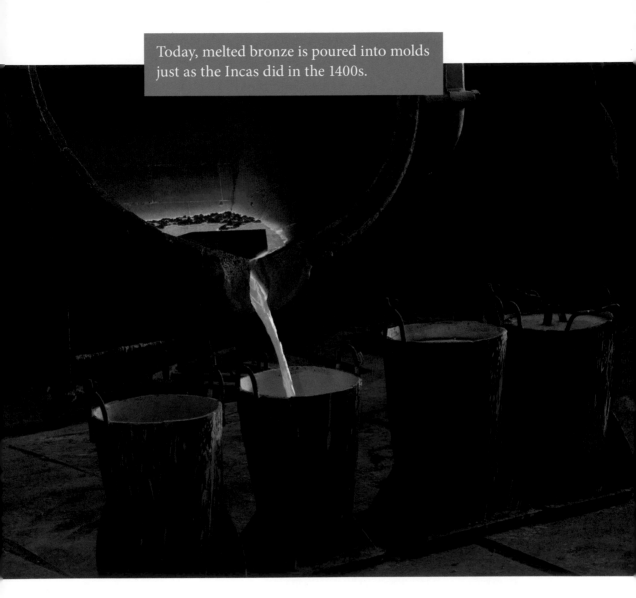

Today, melted bronze is poured into molds just as the Incas did in the 1400s.

MACHU PICCHU'S PEOPLE

In 1912, scientists found more than 100 skeletons at Machu Picchu. At the time, they believed they had found mostly females. The skeletons appeared small in size.

In 2003, scientists studied the skeletons using a modern scientific method involving isotopes. Every chemical element, such as carbon, contains one or more isotopes. Isotopes are atoms with the same number of protons and electrons. They have a different number of neutrons.

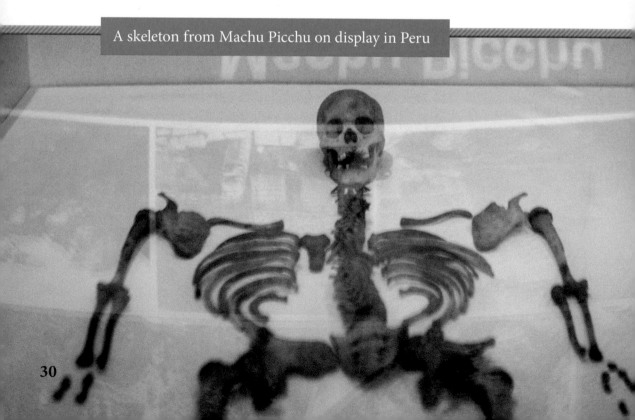

A skeleton from Machu Picchu on display in Peru

Isotopes found in bones can reveal a person's diet, age, sex, and where they lived. These clues help scientists learn more about a person, including their **ethnicity** and overall health. Scientists learned the Machu Picchu skeletons were actually a mix of males and females.

The scientists also looked for chemical traces of foods in bone samples. They found a large amount of chemicals that are usually found in corn. The scientists realized corn was the main food at Machu Picchu. This also meant the site was probably a royal estate. During the Inca empire, only royal members and their servants ate corn.

Isotopes

Carbon is one of the elements scientists look for when using isotopes to learn about ancient people.

CARBON-12
6 neutrons + 6 protons = 12

CARBON-13
7 neutrons + 6 protons = 13

CARBON-14
8 neutrons + 6 protons = 14

Scientists noted that the people of Machu Picchu likely had strong arms and hands. The skeletons had no signs of injury or joint swelling. These people had not taken part in heavy labor or battles. They were likely servants. They had done tasks such as metalworking, cooking, and farming.

It is believed that many people at Machu Picchu were farmers who grew corn.

The skulls of the Machu Picchu skeletons also were examined. Scientists noticed the skulls were longer and narrower than normal. This is called cranial modification. This practice was common in ancient South America. It was done by wrapping infants' heads tightly with cloth bands to reshape them. The shape of the heads reflected specific ethnic groups or regions.

Many of the skull shapes found were typical of regions outside of Cuzco. Scientists realized that Machu Picchu's population was **diverse**. The people came from all over the Inca empire. Artifacts found with the skeletons also reflect styles from different Inca regions.

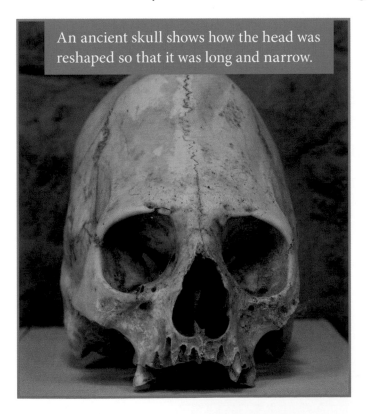
An ancient skull shows how the head was reshaped so that it was long and narrow.

CHAPTER 4

END OF THE INCA EMPIRE

Machu Picchu may have begun with Emperor Pachacuti. However, it did not end with him. Just before he died in 1471, the aging emperor named a new ruler. His son, Tupac Yupanqui, became the next Inca emperor.

Scientists believe that Pachacuti's family continued to live at the citadel. The age of the skeletons and artifacts found there support this idea. In the 1500s, the Spanish conquered South America. This marked the end of the Inca empire. Spanish records reveal that the last Inca emperor fled to Vilcabamba, which was about 50 miles (80 km) west of Machu Picchu. The emperor remained there for 35 years, until the city was destroyed in 1572.

Tupac Yupanqui took over for his father as the emperor of the Inca people.

TUPAC
YVPANQUI
INCAXI.

Despite the Spanish invasion, Machu Picchu may have been abandoned before the Spanish arrived. The Incas were already struggling with civil war. The Incas forced their religion on conquered people. They ruled over them with military force. Some groups resisted Inca rule. The royal Inca family members were also fighting for power among themselves.

At the same time, a deadly disease called smallpox was spreading quickly in the area. Europeans had brought the deadly disease to South America. It was slowly wiping out the Inca and Aztec people. These Native groups had no **immunity** from the disease.

Inca Mummies

Like the ancient Egyptians, the Incas mummified their dead. The exact process is unknown. Dead bodies may have been dried out in hot and cold temperatures before using salt to preserve them. Then they wrapped the bodies in leather, cloth, or natural fibers. Many Inca mummies have been found this way in caves, sitting upright in baskets filled with food and other objects. Mummies were treated as if they were still living. They were brought out of their resting places for feasts, holidays, and parades. No Inca emperor's mummy has ever been found.

By the time the Spanish arrived, the Inca empire was falling apart. Machu Picchu's residents likely left because of disease, civil war, and the threat of Spanish invasion.

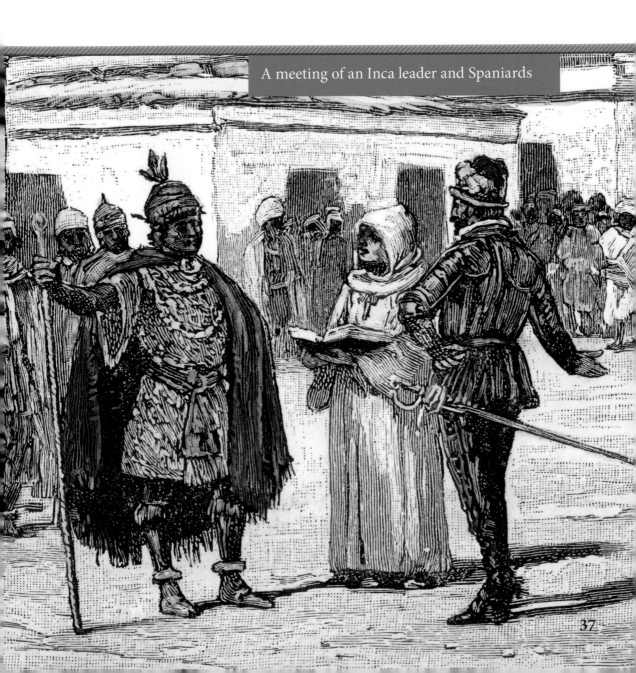

A meeting of an Inca leader and Spaniards

CHAPTER 5

PRESERVING MACHU PICCHU

Today, Machu Picchu is the most visited site in Peru. More than 1 million people visit it every year. Unfortunately, scientists have noted several environmental threats to the site.

Tourists stay in the city of Aguas Calientes, Peru, when they visit Machu Picchu.

Construction and tourism have harmed Machu Picchu and its land. Many hotels and businesses have been built in the region. Construction often requires clearing the land of trees. This can lead to increased flooding and erosion. It also increases water and air pollution.

Chemicals from building materials and equipment are released into the environment. They contain **greenhouse gases** such as carbon dioxide. Greenhouse gases trap the sun's heat. They keep our planet warm and help living things survive. However, farming, construction, manufacturing, and driving have added too many greenhouse gases to the atmosphere. They have increased Earth's temperature. This causes climate change. Warming temperatures make it hard for plants and animals to survive.

Fact

In 1983, Machu Picchu was made a UNESCO World Heritage site. In 2007, it was voted as one of the New Seven Wonders of the World.

Tourism has caused other problems at Machu Picchu. Trash dumping and rock removal cause pollution and erosion. The ancient Inca Trail is also suffering from overuse. People, transport animals, and vehicles wear out the trail. Officials in Peru are working hard to protect the site.

Scientists are trying to understand foot traffic patterns at Machu Picchu. With one method they use infrared sensors to detect movement. Infrared is a type of invisible light energy that can be felt as heat. All objects on Earth let off infrared heat. Infrared sensors can tell when an object has come in its path.

At Machu Picchu, infrared sensors were set up at different locations. Each time a visitor passed through an infrared beam, the data was recorded. That way scientists learned which areas were visited the most.

Scientists know that all the visitors to Machu Picchu have a big impact on the ancient site.

Using other scientific measurements, scientists have come up with new walking routes throughout the site. They have determined how many people visit per day. This data helped Peru's government set new rules for visitors. The number of daily visitors is now limited. People must choose time slots to prevent overcrowding.

In 2020, a project began to lower carbon emissions at Machu Picchu. A large machine removes plastic waste on the Inca Trail. Nearby hotels and restaurants also send used cooking oil to a local energy plant. This plant uses a chemical process to separate the oil from a sugar alcohol called glycerin. The oil becomes a source of clean energy called biodiesel. The glycerin is used to make natural products like soap. This project has helped produce fuel and prevent oil dumping in local rivers.

Waste is loaded on trains to be taken away from Machu Picchu.

Workers clean the stones at Machu Picchu.

Glycerin-based cleaning products are used to clean the citadel. They have taken the place of chemical products. These chemical products could damage Machu Picchu's buildings over time.

Fact
Farming practices such as animal overgrazing and forest burning are also threatening the forest around Machu Picchu.

The organic waste, such as paper, cloth, food, plants, and plastics, collected at the citadel is made into fuel. Through a process called pyrolysis, the waste is heated at a very high temperature. It is heated in a closed space that has no oxygen. Without oxygen, a fire cannot start. For this reason, the waste does not burn. That way it doesn't let carbon into the air. Instead, it turns into environmentally safe oil, gas, and coal.

Visitors separate their trash into different bins for collection.

The bio-coal is added to the soil at Machu Picchu. It helps the soil hold on to water and nutrients while preventing erosion. This soil also supports new tree growth.

Using scientific processes, people can protect Machu Picchu. That way we can enjoy this great legacy of the Inca civilization for years to come.

GLOSSARY

aqueduct (AWK-wuh-dukt)—a structure for carrying water across land

citadel (SIT-uh-del)—a fortress on high ground above a city

descendant (di-SEN-dent)—a person originating or coming from an ancestor

diverse (di-VURS)—including many different types of people or things

emperor (EM-pur-ur)—a male ruler of an empire

ethnicity (eth-NIS-uh-tee)—a particular race of people

excavation (eks-kuh-VAY-shun)—the act of digging the earth to recover old objects buried in the ground

greenhouse gas (GREEN-haus gas)—one of several gases that prevent the earth's heat from escaping into the atmosphere

immunity (ih-MYOO-nuh-tee)—to be protected against disease

microorganism (mye-kroh-OR-gan-iz-uhm)—a living thing that is too small to see without a microscope

nobility (no-BIL-uh-tee)—the people of the highest social rank in a society

quarry (KWEH-ree)—to dig stone

READ MORE

Gale, Ryan. *Your Passport to Peru*. North Mankato, MN: Capstone Press, 2020.

Klepeis, Alicia Z. *Peru*. Minneapolis: Bellwether Media, 2019.

Stine, Megan. *Where Is Machu Picchu?* New York: Penguin Workshop, 2018.

INTERNET SITES

DK Findout! Incas
dkfindout.com/us/history/incas/

Kids Discover: Facts and Theories About Mysterious Machu Picchu
kidsdiscover.com/quick-reads/facts-theories-mysterious-machu-picchu/

National Geographic Kids: Peru
kids.nationalgeographic.com/geography/countries/article/peru

INDEX

ABOUT THE AUTHOR

Golriz Golkar is the author of more than 60 nonfiction books for children. Inspired by her work as an elementary schoolteacher, she loves to write the kinds of books that students are excited to read. Golriz holds a B.A. in American Literature and Culture from UCLA and an Ed.M. in Language and Literacy from the Harvard Graduate School of Education. Golriz lives in France with her husband and young daughter, Ariane.